Celebrating your year

1952

a very special year for

A message from the author:

Welcome to the year 1952.

I trust you will enjoy this fascinating romp down memory lane.

And when you have reached the end of the book, please join me in the battle against AI generated copy-cat books and fake reviews.

Details are at the back of the book.*

Best regards,
Bernard Bradforsand-Tyler.

Contents

1952 American Family Life 8
Austerity in the United Kingdom 13
Death of a Monarch 17
Our Love Affair with Cars 20
The Golden Age of Television 24
Most Popular TV Shows of 1952 25
Birth of the Morning TV Show 29
First Hydrogen Bomb Dropped 31
Korean War Intensifies 32
The Great Smog of London 34
Coup d'État in Egypt 37
Apartheid Laws in South Africa 38
1952 in Cinema and Film 42
Top Grossing Films of the Year 43
1952 Sci-Fi Inspired Films 45
The Chronicles of Narnia 47
Musical Memories 48
1952 Billboard Top 30 Songs 50
Fashion Trends of the 1950s 54
1952 Olympic Games 64
Other Sporting Events from 1952 66
Technology and Medicine 67
Other News from 1952 68
Famous People Born in 1952 72
1952 in Numbers 76
Image Attributions 84

Advertisement

"So lifelike you feel you're right there with 3 dimension pictures!"

New sensational Revere 3 Dimension Camera enables you to take amazing lifelike pictures as easy as pie! Just press the button as you do with any ordinary camera. What you see, you catch in thrilling three dimensions. Everything has shape, form, depth! Full color scenes seem to spring to life with breath-taking 3 dimensional realism. So truly lifelike, viewers exclaim it's like being right there!

See the two lenses? They're perfectly matched and act like your eyes. Simply press the button and they take two separate views of each scene. When viewed, they blend into 3 dimensions. Inexpensive, too! Get 29 stereos from regular 35mm roll; 20 from special stereo film.

Even beginners get fine results from their first roll, so simple is Revere to operate! Guesswork is eliminated. Even focusing for distance is automatic with the built-in range finder. Stereos are now mounted by your film processor and are returned to you ready to show!

Every picture is a thrill! Sheer enjoyment when you view stereos through the new Revere Viewer. Advance design brings out the best in every shot. Ask your dealer to show you the new Revere Stereo Camera and Viewer.

For a new adventure in photography... Revere 33 Stereo Camera

Let's flashback to 1952, a very special year.

Was this the year you were born?

Was this the year you were married?

Whatever the reason, this book is a celebration of your year,

THE YEAR 1952.

Turn the pages to discover a book packed with fun-filled fabulous facts. We look at the people, the places, the politics and the pleasures that made 1952 unique and helped shape the world we know today.

So get your time-travel suit on, and enjoy this trip down memory lane, to rediscover what life was like, back in the year 1952.

1952 American Family Life

Imagine if time-travel was a reality, and one fine morning you wake up to find yourself flashed back in time, back to the year 1952.

What would life be like for a typical family, in a typical town, somewhere in America?

Artist's impression of a typical children's birthday party around the TV set in the 1950s.

The post-war boom continued throughout the entire decade of the '50s. And with the booming economy, came booming birth numbers, booming suburbs, and the booming trappings of the consumerist culture we still live in today.

Our rising middle classes were feeling cashed-up. With an increasing desire to spend and to own, consumer demand continued to reach new highs year after year.

An unprecedented 3.89 million babies were born in 1952 (up from 2.8 million at the end of the war seven years earlier).[1]

To cater to the increase in demand, new houses were built in record numbers, most of them in the new suburban developments springing up on the outskirts of towns. Home sales were boosted by returned soldiers who had access to low interest loans through the G.I. Bill (1944-1956). A house in the suburbs had become the American dream for white middle-class families.

The family was everything. Fathers commuted to earn a salary. Wives were encouraged to quit their jobs and stay at home. Children walked to school and played outdoors in their well manicured gardens.

Families dined together, watched television together, and enjoyed leisure time and outings together.

Average costs in 1952 [4]	
New house	$9,050
New car	$1,700
Clothes washer	$150
Refrigerator	$440
A gallon of gasoline	$0.27

Relaxing in the sun in 1952 American suburbs.

The average family income was $3,900 a year.[2] Unemployment had dropped to 2.7%, with GDP growth at 4.1%.[3]

[1] U.S. Census Bureau *Estimates of the Population of the United States*: 1950-1954, page 2.
[2] census.gov/library/publications/1954/demo/p60-015.html.
[3] thebalance.com/unemployment-rate-by-year-3305506.
[4] thepeoplehistory.com and mclib.info/reference/local-history-genealogy/historic-prices/.

Advertisement

All shelves roll out in the new Cycla-matic Frigidaire.
Just what you've been waiting for to replace your obsolete refrigerator.

SEE this big, true food freezer! Completely sealed off, completely insulated – with its own cold-making system. Keeps every pound of food fresh and firm for months at a time, in absolute zero-zone safety.

SEE the only heatless automatic defrosting! Cycla-matic defrosting is the newest, simplest of them all! Not only banishes frost before it collects, but gives you positive moisture control at the same time. And does it without adding heat!

SEE exclusive Levelcold – produced by the Meter-Miser! No more see-saw temperatures! No more "hot spots" or "cold spots." Fresh foods keep beautifully on any shelf. And there's a separate thermostat outside as well as inside, so constant temperatures are maintained regardless of where you place the Cycla-matic Frigidaire.

SEE all the shelves roll out – all the way! See the aluminium shelves that cannot rust, glide out all the way – putting every ounce of food right at your finger tips! In no other make of refrigerator can this be done! Shelves on the door, too, for added storage space. It's wonderful!

Finest of 15 million Frigidaires Cycla-matic Frigidaire

Joining the television in our families' list of must-haves were: fully-automatic washing machines, front-loading dryers, defrost refrigerators, vacuum cleaners, air-conditioning and heating units, milkshake makers, and a multitude of other kitchen gadgets and fancy home appliances. In addition, every respectable family needed a car or two, motorcycles, bicycles, hiking/ camping/ picnic gear, and much, much more. An energetic and persuasive advertising industry, through TV, radio and print, ensured we always knew what our next purchase should be.

A Hotpoint dishwasher magazine advertisement from 1952.

A safety education magazine cover from the '50s.

But beneath the appearance of abundance and domestic bliss, Americans were deeply concerned. The Soviets had detonated an atomic bomb in 1949, setting in motion a nuclear race between the two superpowers—the Cold War.

By the end of 1952, the USA would succeed in their quest to build an even more powerful weapon—the hydrogen bomb.

We would endure nearly four more decades of tension between the two super-powers before the Cold War finally ended with the dissolution of the Soviet Union in 1991.

Advertisement

Even Bud forgot the pie!

More families buy World Book than any other Encyclopedia

1ˢᵗ Choice of America's schools and libraries. *Ask any teacher or librarian.*

Even Bud forgot the pie!

Table talk had centered around the presidential election. Then Nancy asked, "Dad, how does the electoral college work?" "Well, er" said Dad. "It…" "Hey," chimed in Bud, "Let's look it up in the World Book!" Soon the discussion turned to democracy, and World Book's fascinating article on "government" was in the thick of it. Bud read parts of it aloud and everyone joined in the discussion. Mom brought in the pie unnoticed. World Book had provided such fascinating food for thought that even Bud forgot the pie!…

Your family, too, will find in World Book Encyclopedia an unending source of accurate information, beautifully presented. Whether it's politics or paintings, animals or atoms, transportation or textiles… World Book provides the authoritative facts in fascinating text and pictures.

Better school grades in an amazingly short time – that's the report of 9 out of 10 families who have given their children the advantages of World Book in the home. It helps develop the habit of learning which leads to the habit of success.

More families buy World Book than any other Encyclopedia
1ˢᵗ Choice of America's schools and libraries. Ask any teacher or librarian.

Austerity in the United Kingdom

Now just imagine you flashed back to a town in 1952 United Kingdom or Western Europe.

Unlike boom-time America, a very different, more restrained lifestyle would await you.

For the British, 1952 was a year marked by two events of extreme collective sadness and suffering. The year started with the death of their beloved King, plunging the country into a period of mourning. The year finished with a toxic smog blanketing London, so severe an estimated 10,000-12,000 died from smog related illnesses. It would become known as "The Great Smog".

These events added to the ongoing distress endured in the aftermath of the war. But to lighten their hearts, the Brits welcomed a new Queen, and after 13 years, the rationing of tea was lifted.

Indian Test cricketer Probir Sen shakes hands with Queen Elizabeth II at Lord's Cricket Ground in London, 23rd June 1952.

London, like many other major European cities, bore the brunt of destruction from WWII bombings. Reconstruction was painfully slow, hampered by a general shortage of money, manpower and materials.

In cities there was a desperate shortage of housing to accommodate the growing population. Nearly half of those in cities lived in private, rented, often substandard apartments. While in the country, homes often lacked water, sanitation, electricity and phones.

Aerial view of London showing bombed areas in the foreground, 1953.

Stifling and miserable austerity measures, in place since the start of the war, were slowly being lifted. By 1952, most items were available for purchase without coupons, however rationing of sugar and meat would continue for a couple more years.

The post-war baby boom, along with the shortage of funds and building materials for new schools, often resulted in crowded classes of up to 50 students in urban areas.

British children at school in the early '50s.

Sir Winston Churchill, UK Prime Minister from 1940-1945, won the general election of October 1951 to be reinstalled for an additional four years. He wasted no time traveling to the USA for talks with President Truman, arriving in New York on 5th January 1952. The purpose of Churchill's visit was to renew UK's "special relationship" with America, and to discuss joint strategies for communism containment.

Harry Truman and Winston Churchill, 1952.

This "special relationship" hinged not only on the two countries' common distrust of communism, but also recognized the financial assistance the US had provided a bankrupt Britain following the war. The substantial loans were finally paid back in full in the year 2006.

Lack of excess cash reserves made it increasingly difficult for the UK to continue financing and keeping secure its far-flung colonies. As a result, many British colonies would be released during the following 10 years, gaining independence as new nations. The United Kingdom was quickly losing its super-power status on the world's stage.

Advertisement

All over America _ Smokers are changing to Chesterfield

"Chesterfields are provided exclusively on all United's Strato-cruiser flights to Honolulu. We have found our passengers prefer Chesterfields." [signed] Vice President, United Air Lines.

Dale Robertson gets his Chesterfields from Stewardess Audrey Jones. See him starring in "Lydia Bailey." A 20th Century-Fox Production. Color by Technicolor.

Wherever you go- Sound Off for Mildness _ plus No Unpleasant After-taste* *from the report of a well-known research organization. ... And Only Chesterfield Has It! Try Them Today!

Death of a Monarch

6th February 1952

On 6th Feb, the British populace woke to the news that their beloved monarch, King George VI, had died peacefully in his sleep. He was 56 years old. Flags were lowered to half mast, parliament suspended, TV broadcasts canceled, cinemas and theatres closed in his honor.

The King's death, caused by a blood clot, was sudden and unexpected, even though he was known to be in rather poor health. Years of heavy smoking had left him with lung cancer, requiring the removal of his entire left lung five months earlier.

Born second in line to the throne, King George VI had become monarch after the abdication of his older brother in 1936. Although his reign was short, he was incredibly popular.

King George VI, circa 1942.

Queen Elizabeth II, 1959.

The King's funeral was held on 15th February. Several foreign monarchs and leaders attended the service. He was buried in the royal vault of the chapel at Windsor Castle.

King George VI was survived by his wife, who lived another 50 years as The Queen Mother, and his two daughters, Elizabeth and Margaret.

Elizabeth, on tour in Zimbabwe at the time, immediately ascended to the throne on the same day as her father's passing, becoming Queen Elizabeth II.

Advertisement

A stand-out in style! Saves gas every mile!
Studebaker Starliner
America's Smartest "Hard-Top"

This excitingly different Studebaker "hard-top" can be yours as a sprightly Champion in the lowest price field – or, if you wish, as a brilliantly-powered Commander V-8.

Sparkling with verve and vigor in every line, it's a remarkable gas saver. That's because Studebaker designing keeps it free from power-wasting excess weight.

Stop in at a dealer's showroom as soon as you can. Try out a Starliner or one of the other thrilling new Studebakers.

Studebaker Automatic Drive or Overdrive is available in all models at extra cost.

'52 Studebaker.

Advertisement

In a realm all its own... Cadillac

In all the world of commerce, there are a few products for which there are no acceptable substitutes. And among these, most certainly, must be counted the great Cadillac car. For in beauty and elegance...in luxury and comfort...in value and practicality...in everything that contributes to making a motor car supreme—Cadillac is in a realm all its own. To see it and to drive it is to discover a new measure of fulfillment in modern motoring. Your Cadillac dealer will be most happy to demonstrate this fact to you at any time—and to explain why Cadillac is now such an unusually sound investment for such a surprisingly wide group of motorists. We hope you will accord him the opportunity—soon.

In a realm all its own... Cadillac

Our Love Affair with Cars

In the seven years since war's end, the US car industry had shifted from fabricating utilitarian war tanks and trucks, to producing fashionable consumer vehicles, the kind of which we just had to have.

There were now 43.7 million registered cars on US roads, up from 25.7 million at the end of WWII.[1] Our love affair with cars was firmly entrenched.

Mid-Afternoon Traffic on Broad Street, Philadelphia, early '50s.

Detroit had long been the car manufacturing hub of the country, and America led the world in car production, turning out 6 million vehicles in 1952 alone.[2]

Detroit's population had peaked two years earlier, making it the fifth largest city in the US.[3] And by the end of the decade, a whopping one in six adults nation-wide would be employed in the car industry.

[1] fhwa.dot.gov/ohim/summary95/mv200.pdf.
[2] en.wikipedia.org/wiki/American_automobile_industry_in_the_1950s.
[3] theweek.com/articles/461968/rise-fall-detroit-timeline.

1952 Hudson Hornet Hollywood Hardtop.

Our love affair with cars grew hand-in-hand with the post-war baby boom and housing construction boom. Where would we be without our cars? How else could we commute from our outer-suburban homes to our inner-city offices?

Rising incomes ensured the family car was increasingly affordable. An additional 1.13 million vehicles were put on US roads during 1952 as families fled the cities for the quiet life of the suburbs.

Cars were no longer just a necessity; they had become an expression of our personality. Sturdy, sporty, or luxurious, cars now came in a wide range of styles, colors, and price points, with chrome, wings, stripes and fins for added personality.

Advertisement

"but darling... they're staring at our new '52 Dodge"
Drive the very new, very beautiful '52 Dodge.
Enjoy greater all 'round visibility, smoother riding, extra roominess, the pride and satisfaction of having spent your money wisely and well.
Big, new, dependable '52 Dodge.

Advertisement

Lincoln invites you to try modern living in action

You have to live with modern living to appreciate it. You have to be inside a glass-walled home to know its comfort and luxury and outdoor spaciousness.

And that is the way it is with a Lincoln. It is modern living on wheels. To understand it fully you have to get in...and drive. You must experience its cat-like maneuverability in crowded places, on tight turns. You must learn, firsthand, that an American fine car can combine a soft-cushioning ride with a lively sportscar "cornering" agility. So accept our invitation to a drive. For only by living with a Lincoln can you know this magnificent new concept of the fine car. A new Lincoln Cosmopolitan or Capri is ready for your test at your Lincoln dealer. Tomorrow, you can be behind the wheel of *the one fine car deliberately designed for modern living.*

Take a day with modern living in motion. Experience the thrill of Lincoln's completely new high compression overhead valve V-S engine. How effortless—with dual range Hydra-Matic Transmission (standard equipment) and with exclusive new ball-joint front wheel suspension.

Broad view on life. Only behind the wheel of a Lincoln can you really appreciate the unobstructed view of the road ahead. The big, wide, safety-curve windshield does it for you. Look around...see how its glass-walled visibility gives you a panoramic look of the outdoors (up to 3,271 square inches of glass).

The Golden Age of Television

During the '50s, the television set quickly became the centerpiece of every family home. By 1952, 15.3 million American households, equivalent to 34.2% of the population, owned a television set, (an increase of nearly 50% from just 12 months earlier).[1] And that number would rise exponentially throughout the decade as television became our preferred choice of entertainment.

Family focused Motorola television advertisements from 1952.

For the rising middle classes, television was much more convenient than going to a downtown cinema. It provided an increasing array of programs to watch, was available every day of the week, and it was free to watch once purchased.

The rise of television spelt doom for the motion-picture industry. Cinema going audiences deserted downtown movie theaters in droves, forcing many to close.

[1] americancentury.omeka.wlu.edu/items/show/136.

Most Popular Television Shows of 1952

1. I Love Lucy
2. Arthur Godfrey's Talent Scouts
3. Arthur Godfrey and His Friends
4. Dragnet
5. Texaco Star Theater
6. The Buick Circus Hour
7. The Colgate Comedy Hour
8. Gangbusters
9. You Bet Your Life
10. Fireside Theatre
11. The Red Buttons Show
12. The Jack Benny Show
13. Life with Luigi
14. Pabst Blue Ribbon Bouts
15. Goodyear TV Playhouse
16. The Life of Riley
17. Philco TV Playhouse
18. Mama
19. Your Show of Shows
20. What's My Line?
    = Strike It Rich

* Nielsen Media Research 1952-'53 season of top-rated primetime television series in the USA.

In the early '50s, television continued to rely on live broadcasts of popular radio programs. These were faster and cheaper to produce than new made-for-TV dramas.

Comedy-Varieties remained our most popular form of family-time TV entertainment, accounting for 5 of the top 7 programs for the year.

Dean Martin and Jerry Lewis in *The Colgate Comedy Hour* (NBC. 1950-1955).

Also keeping us glued to our screens were highly rated drama series such as *Dragnet* (NBC. 1951-'59), *Fireside Theater* (NBC. 1949-'58), *Philco TV Playhouse* (NBC. 1948-'55), and *Goodyear TV Playhouse* (NBC. 1951-'57).

Jack Webb (Sergeant Joe Friday) and Harry Morgan in *Dragnet* (NBC. 1951-1959).

Kinder to Your Eyes

HaloLight, for Greater Viewing Comfort, comes only in

SYLVANIA TV

Conventional Picture

Kinder to Your Eyes
HaloLight

Kinder to Your Eyes
HaloLight, for Greater Viewing Comfort, comes only in Sylvania TV.

HaloLight, the new exclusive Sylvania development for greater viewing comfort, surrounds the picture screen with a cool frame of light. HaloLight ends the sharp contrast between the bright picture screen and the dark surroundings. Actually makes the picture look larger, seem clearer. Your eyes will thank you for HaloLight.

HaloLight is only one of the many exclusive television features in a television set manufactured by Sylvania, pioneers for 50 years in the development of lighting and electronics. For the finest reception in television today and television to come, be sure—select Sylvania.

The Jefferson–20" Life-size Movie-Class television receiver with HaloLight. Hepplewhite cabinet with hand-rubbed finish. Console with doors finished in delicate marquetry.

Sylvania. Established 1901–Great Name in Electronics

Teenagers dancing on *American Bandstand* (WFIL. 1952-'56, ABC. 1956-'87).

Herb Nelson, Ellen Demming, Susan Douglas, and Lyle Sudrow in *The Guiding Light* (CBS. 1952-2009).

The television networks were quick to turn out new programs to keep us tuning in. Here are just a few of the new programs that aired for the first time in 1952: *American Bandstand* (37 seasons), *The Guiding Light* (57 seasons), *I've Got a Secret*, *This Is Your Life*, *The Adventures of Ozzie and Harriet*, and *The Today Show* (1952-present).

This is Your Life original host Ralph Edwards with guest Lillian Roth (NBC. 1952-'61).

The Today Show original host Dave Garroway with friends (NBC. 1952-present).

Advertisement

...and Best of All —a PHILCO!

Multiwave PHILCO
Radio with Sensational
Special Service Band

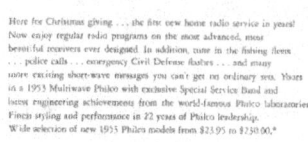

...and Best of All—a Philco! Multiwave Philco Radio with Sensational Special Service Band.

Here for Christmas giving... the first new home radio service in years! Now enjoy regular radio programs on the most advanced, most beautiful receivers ever designed. In addition, tune in the fishing fleets... police calls... emergency Civil Defense flashes... and many more exciting short-wave messages you can't get on ordinary sets. Yours in a 1952 Multiwave Philco with exclusive Special Service Band and latest engineering achievements from the world-famous Philco laboratories. Finest styling and performance in 22 years of Philco leadership.
Wide selection of new 1953 Philco models from $23.95 to $230.00.

Philco Famous for Quality the World Over.

• TV-Convertible Radio-Phonograph! Drop-leaf top accomodates television table model, Philco 1750. • Exclusive! Radio-Phonograph with the first pick-up to reproduce the full range of harmonics. Philco 1350. • New Gift ideas! Combination lamp and automatic clock-radio—plus Special Service Band. Philco 706. • Worldwide Reception! The finiest radio ever built for the American public... 9 tuning bands. Philco 960. • Aristocrat of all automatic clock-radios... with exclusive Philco Special Service Band. Philco 804. • Give America's Finest portable... luxury styled in rich cowhide finish case. Philco Multiwave 658. • Decorator Styling at its best... with performance to match. Philco 950 in Ivory or Mahogany finish. • Anyone will be thrilled with this dramatically new Philco 563. Modern Ebony or Swedish Red cabinet.

Birth of the Morning TV Show

14th January 1952

When NBC aired *The Today Show* on the morning of 14th January, a new genre of TV programming was born. David Garroway told viewers they would now leave the house "knowing where you're going and what the world is like that you're going into". The show introduced the concept of a morning update for news, weather, gossip, and light banter, with live reports from far flung places.

Garroway was authentic, talking to us without reading or shouting, a welcome part of our morning routine.

Garroway with his familiar sign off, palm raised while he said "Peace".

Garroway and crew on *The Today Show* set, 1952.

Instead of waiting for prime-time programs in the late afternoon, viewers now had a reason to turn on their TV sets in the morning. And those sets tended to stay on for the whole day. The rise of television consumption expanded exponentially, and with it the advertising dollars, which financed new sitcoms, dramas, news, and other novel broadcasts.

Producer Sylvester "Pat" Weaver imagined an alternative to morning radio, where viewers could listen while dressing, shaving, and eating breakfast. He also lobbied for programs to have multiple advertising sponsors instead of just one, as was the norm, to prevent sponsors gaining control over program content. His NBC executives were skeptical, arguing that no-one would watch TV in the morning.

Weaver was a true television pioneer, creating the formula that is still followed by morning shows of today.

Advertisement

Now-gorgeous color movies ...simpler, surer, ...so easy to afford

Someday, you've promised yourself, you'd put your family "in the movies." With Kodak's budget-priced movie cameras, that "someday" is here! Back-yard barbecue... and all the other specially happy times are yours to keep in movies you make yourself.

So truly themselves... home movies capture the familiar expressions... the smiles and gestures that are your dear ones. There's no trick to it... and the results are wonderful. Today, home movies are so simple even a child can make them! Done to a turn. Snapshot-easy home movies capture the glorious color... the vibrant reality of life itself.

You can have your steak and eat it, too. Movies bring back all the fun and excitement... the very essence of your good times. The parties... the celebrations... the days that mean most spring to life whenever you wish... on your movie screen. Perfect ending... that will last for years. Movies are so inexpensive over a million families enjoy them regularly.

This year there's a Brownie Movie Camera for only $43.30.

It's Kodak's new Brownie Movie Camera that loads and shoots as easily as your faithful "box Brownie"...gets crisp, clear movies with true Brownie ease. Film costs are low, too. You can make the movie you see here...in seven full-length movie scenes in full color...for under a dollar, complete! Easy to make, to afford, to get started—that's home movies the easy Kodak way.

- Brownie Movie Camera, 8mm. (left) with f/2.7 lens, $43.30. • Cine-Kodak Magazine 8 Camera (right) with f/1.9 lens, 3-second loading, slow-motion setting, $150.95.

First Hydrogen Bomb Dropped 1ˢᵗ November 1952

Cold War tensions between the two former allies–the USSR and the USA–dominated our lives throughout the '50s and '60s. Starting in the USA as policies for communist containment, the distrust and misunderstanding between the two sides quickly escalated from political squabbling, to a military nuclear arms race. For more than 40 years, the Nuclear Arms Race gave the two superpowers the pretext needed to test nuclear bombs on a massive scale.

After 7 years of testing atomic (fission) bombs on land, sea and air, the USA flexed its nuclear might by detonating the world's first hydrogen (thermonuclear fusion) bomb in Enewetak Atoll, in the Pacific Ocean. Code-named *Ivy Mike*, it weighed about 82 tons and yielded 10 megatons.

Ivy Mike atmospheric nuclear test, 1ˢᵗ Nov 1952.

The mushroom cloud created by Ivy Mike rose 41 km (25.5 mi), with a radius spreading out 161 km (100 mi). The heavily contaminated area saw radioactive coral rain down on ships as far as 56 km (35 mi) away.

Las Vegas tourist postcard, circa 1951.

One hour after detonation, US Air Force pilots flew into the cloud to take radioactive samples. Conditions were dangerous, with little or no protective clothing, poor visibility, extreme heat, flying debris, and electromagnetic interference on flight equipment. One pilot was lost to the sea, his body never recovered.

More than 2,000 nuclear bombs have been tested since 1945, with millions of people unwittingly exposed to radioactive fallout over the years.

Korean War Intensifies 1950-1953

American forces entered the Korean War in 1950, joined by a UN combined force from twenty-one countries including the UK, Australia, Canada, France, Philippines, and Thailand. Their purpose was to assist South Korea with expelling communist invaders from the north. In contrast to the well equipped and well trained North Korean military (KPA), the South Korean forces were ill prepared and outnumbered.

By the start of 1952, both sides were exhausted by the relentless battles. While the UN allies fought for a return to the Post War status quo of two Koreas divided along the 38th Parallel, the KPA was determined to unite Korea as one country under communist rule.

Medical corpsmen helping wounded infantrymen, following the fight for Hill 598, 14th Oct 1952.

M4A3E8 "Sherman" Tank of Company B, 72nd Tank Battalion, 2nd Infantry Division, on "Napalm Ridge", 11th May 1952.

With military backing from China and financial aid from the Soviets, the KPA crossed the 38th parallel, capturing Seoul five times during the first 10 months of war. Each offensive was followed by a retreat, being pushed back by the UN allies towards to the border with China.

An ongoing stalemate held throughout 1952, with multiple battles of attrition waged, resulting in little or no progress on the ground.

In the air however, UN forces exploited their superior military power, dominating the skies. The US supplied much needed rocket launchers, anti-aircraft guns, jets, and bombers. US pilots conducted night-time bomb raids, venturing deeper and deeper into North Korea to destroy enemy targets.

Soldiers boarding a U.S. Army Sikorsky H-19 Chickasaw helicopter.

A total of 635,000 tons of bombs were dropped on North Korea, turning nearly every city and village to rubble. Citizens were advised to dig tunnels to live in.

In addition, the US dropped 32,557 tons of lethal napalm.

A U.S. Navy McDonnell F2H-2 Banshee of Fighter Squadron 11 (VF-11). 20th Oct 1952.

Casualties of war saw an estimated 1.68 million South Korean lives lost. Food shortages and lack of housing were severe.

Casualties for the North Koreans and Chinese were even higher.

Korean girl carrying her baby brother walks by a stalled M-46 tank at Haengju, 9th June 1950.

An estimated 3 million people lost their lives during the war, of which half were civilians from both South and North Korea. Causes of death included bombings, massacres, starvation and disease.

The war unofficially ended in July 1953 with the creation of the Demilitarized Zone separating the two Koreas. To date no peace treaty has been signed, leaving the two Koreas technically still at war.

The Great Smog of London

5th–9th December 1952

The Great Smog of 1952 was the deadliest air pollution event ever recorded in the history of the United Kingdom. An estimated 10,000 to 12,000 Londoners died during the five days of intense smog, and from smog related health complications during the months that followed.

London's "pea soupers" had plagued the city for centuries. The yellowish smog (smoke and fog combined), laden with sulfur dioxide and other industrial pollutants, had been captured by artists and recorded in the writings of Charles Dickens and other writers as far back as the 13th Century.

Londoners had become accustomed to the recurring smog, which worsened as the population grew and industrialization expanded. Over the centuries, little had been done to improve the air quality.

Big Ben seen during the Great Smog, 1952.

Battersea Power Station in 1950.

By 1952, 90% of British power was supplied by coal. Several coal-fired power stations and city factories remained in central London, belching toxic sulfur-laden smoke from their chimneys. Pollutants from domestic fireplaces, vehicle exhaust and heavy industry added to the lethal mix.

In December 1952, a period of intense cold weather forced Londoners to burn more coal than usual to stay warm. Smoke particulates mixed with the winter fog causing an extreme smog event which became known as "the Great Smog of London".

An unusual high-pressure anticyclone kept the lethal smog trapped at ground level for five full days. Visibility was so poor that trains and traffic came to a stand still. Unable to see more than an arm's length, people abandoned their cars on the street and shuffled home.

Hospitals filled with patients suffering from bronchitis and pneumonia. Death and complications from respiratory tract and lung infections continued for months after the smog lifted.

Aerial view of Big Ben and the Houses of Parliament during the Great Smog of 1952 (top image) and on a clear day, 2013.

Parliament was finally pressured to act for the health and wellbeing of the citizens. New legislation came about as a result of the deadly smog—one of the first pieces of environmental policy created anywhere in the world. Within four years, the *Clean Air Act* of 1956 mandated the replacement of coal-burning fires with gas or electric heating. Heavy industry and power stations would be moved out of cities, and tall chimney stacks would be fitted with internal pollutant scrubbers.

Advertisement

O'er the ramparts we watch as we track a guided missile aimed at an attacking enemy or his home base. Yes, missiles may fight tomorrow's battles or prevent them. And Convair, the only company developing and building every basic type of aircraft, has a guided missile team helping America achieve a weapons system for every conceivable mission. Watch for new ramparts of peace, built through engineering that aims at the maximum of power... the Nth Power!

CONVAIR

Coup d'État in Egypt

23rd July 1952

The military coup that toppled the reign of King Farouk of Egypt was much more than a power-grab by a band of fractious army officers. It marked the start of a wave of political change across the Arab world, ousting colonial powers and corrupt monarchies, laying foundations for Arab nationalism, independence and solidarity.

On 23rd July, the leaders of the Free Officers Movement began arresting known royalist commanders to gain control of all military units. They announced the coup at 7.30am via a radio broadcast read by Anwar Sadat, the future President of Egypt.

Crowds gathered in the streets to celebrate the end of King Farouk's rule. The King was quickly escorted to Italy, where he remained in exile until his death in 1965.

Prime Minister Gamal Abdel Nasser welcomed by cheering crowds in Alexandria after the signing of the British withdrawal order in 1954.

President Muhammad Naguib (left) & Prime Minister Nasser (right), 1954.

The revolutionaries rounded up corrupt politicians for trial, redistributed British or European owned land, and created a new constitution based on the ideal of a socialist Arab state.

On 18th June 1953, the Monarchy was officially abolished, and the Republic of Egypt formed with General Mohamed Naguib as its first President.

Apartheid Laws in South Africa

By 1952, the Afrikaner National Party had been in power in South Africa for four years. Their policies of "apartheid" (apartness), based on white supremacist ideals, divided non-whites along color and tribal lines. The following years saw numerous Acts come into effect, to strengthen apartheid laws and reinforce white minority rule.

The voting rights of blacks and mixed-race were removed. Interracial marriage or sex was prohibited. Access to schools and other facilities were separately designated. Even access to employment was controlled. The creation of the Group Areas Act (1950) and the Prevention of Illegal Squatting Act (1951) ensured 80% of the land was reserved for exclusive ownership by the ruling white minority.

These Acts allowed for forcible, often violent, removal of non-whites from white designated areas. Evictions of entire suburbs, destruction of property, fines and criminal arrests became commonplace over the following decades.

Area warning signs were commonplace.

To control the movement of black citizens, the decades-old Pass Laws were strengthened. The Black (Natives) Laws Amendment Act (1952) and the Pass Laws Act (1952) stipulated where, when, and for how long a black person could remain in a white neighborhood. Every black person over 16 years of age was required to carry a "passbook" at all times and ensure a valid entry stamp to remain in a white designated area. Failure to do so could result in arrest and imprisonment.

On 26th June, Nelson Mandela, Walter Sisulu, and fifty other activists commenced a public defiance of apartheid laws movement known as the Defiance Campaign. All marched without permits. All were arrested. The campaign spread nationwide and by mid-December, a total of 8,057 protestors had been arrested.

Membership of anti-apartheid organizations skyrocketed as a direct result of the Defiance Campaign, bringing the unjust racial system to the attention of the United Nations and the world.

Protest marches and arrests in South Africa in the early '50s.

The apartheid laws were strengthened and amended multiple times over subsequent years. Following decades of international condemnation and sanctions, the laws were finally repealed in 1991 with the dismantling of South Africa's apartheid system.

Advertisement

Hawaii gets regular air service from five west coast cities. And even from the east coast, it's less than a day away! Giant DC-6 airplanes continue on from Hawaii to Australia, the Philippines and India.

Less than a day away—by Air!

• Switzerland is now a mere 14 hours from New York by the big, modern Douglas DC-6. Be there for the winter sports. "Thrift Season" fairs save you money! • Britain is overnight by air. A businessman can fly to London, spend several days and fly home—in the time it takes to get there by sea! Tons of cargo fly, too; saves on inventory costs, packing, insurance. • Peru is now entering its delightful spring season. Soon it will be summer below the equator—an ideal time to travel. Fly down South America's west coast, return up the east coast. Unforgettable! • The Netherlands can easily be included in your air trip to Europe. Plan on it!... For free, expert help in arranging any trip, ask any of the airlines listed at the right. Or see a travel agent. • World's most modern airplane—Today. 79% of Douglas production is military. But new DC-6's are being built for the airlines, too. The big Douglas DC-6, most modern civilian airplane in the skies today, has carried over 20 million people on these leading airlines of the world.

Twice as many people fly Douglas as all other airplanes combined.

Advertisement

She's dialing California from Englewood, N.J.

An entirely new kind of Long Distance service is now being tried in Englewood, New Jersey. Ten thousand telephone customers in that city now dial their own calls to certain distant points. It's easy to do and faster. Just by dialing two or three more digits than on a local call, they can reach any one of eleven million telephones in and around twelve cities from coast to coast.

This new way of putting through Long Distance calls is another example of the way Bell System people are constantly planning and building to provide you with better telephone service. First comes the idea. Next the inventing, manufacturing and trial in actual use. Then, as soon as possible, the extension of the improved service to more and more people.

Helpful hint—Keep a list of Long Distance numbers handy beside your telephone. Out-of-town calls go through faster when you Call By Number.

Bell Telephone System

1952 in Cinema and Film

Filming of a scene from *The Greatest Show on Earth* (Paramount Pictures, 1952).

Highest Paid Stars

1. Dean Martin & Jerry Lewis
2. Gary Cooper
3. John Wayne
4. Bing Crosby
5. Bob Hope
6. James Stewart
7. Doris Day

Having reached its peak in the mid-1940s, cinema attendance faced a steady decline throughout the 1950s. With more and more families filling their leisure time with the convenience of television, the motion-picture industry sought new ways to win over new audiences.

Younger audiences now had cash to spare. Movie themes adjusted to accommodate the trends in popular culture, and to exploit the sex appeal of young, rising stars such as Marilyn Monroe, James Dean and Marlon Brando.

Dean Martin, Jerry Lewis and Marilyn Monroe at the 1953 Redbook Awards.

Brigitte Bardot, circa 1960.

1952 film debuts

Anne Bancroft	Don't Bother to Knock
Brigitte Bardot	Crazy for Love
Audrey Dalton	My Cousin Rachel
George Hamilton	Lone Star
Henry Silva	Viva Zapata!
Claire Bloom	Limelight

* From en.wikipedia.org/wiki/1952_in_film.

Top Grossing Films of the Year

1	The Greatest Show on Earth	Paramount Pictures	$12,800,000
2	The Snows of Kilimanjaro	20th Century Fox	$6,500,000
3	Hans Christian Andersen	RKO/Samuel Goldwyn	$6,000,000
4	Ivanhoe	MGM	$5,810,000
5	Sailor Beware	Paramount Pictures	$4,300,000
6	Moulin Rouge	United Artists	$4,252,000
7	Jumping Jacks	Paramount Pictures	$4,000,000
8	The Quiet Man	Republic Pictures	$3,800,000
9	Come Back, Little Sheba	Paramount Pictures	$3,500,000
10	High Noon	United Artists	$3,400,000
=	Son of Paleface	Paramount Pictures	$3,400,000

* From en.wikipedia.org/wiki/1952_in_film by box office gross in the USA.

Although not a major box office hit when first released, the musical comedy *Singing in the Rain* (released 27th March 1952) is now widely regarded as one of the greatest movie musicals ever made.

Advertisement

Girls who get ahead know why—

THEY CHOOSE CLOTHES, for instance, that do something *good* for them... clothes to wear at the office, a dress to wear in the evening.

Doesn't it make good "get-ahead" sense to choose your office typewriter in the same way?

Royal Electric, too, does something for you as a secretary who believes, "I'm good. I'm going places."

Royal is the leading make of typewriter. Surveys show it is the brand preferred 2¼ to 1 by girls who type.

Designed with you in mind, the Royal Electric Typewriter is newly engineered throughout. Electricity does the work for you! Tension and fatigue are well-nigh banished... and you *feel* better and *look* better, when five o'clock comes.

You'll *love* its operation! The controls are in the same positions as on your favorite Royal Standard Typewriter. There's virtually no "change-over" problem. Who doesn't like being on familiar ground?

Now, you ask, how about the work? It pours out... literally. As many as 20 carbon copies, too. Your letters sparkle with a crisp clarity that does you credit. Heavy-duty work is delivered with remarkable speed, ease and efficiency.

Exclusive "Touch Control" allows you to adjust the touch to give you the "feel" you prefer. Exclusive "Magic" Margin permits instant, automatic margin setting.

The Royal Electric is *your* typewriter... because of its many exclusive features... because it was designed with *you* in mind. So—do something nice for yourself. Choose Royal.

MAIL TODAY

Royal Typewriter Co., Inc., Dept. F-13
2 Park Avenue, New York 16, N. Y.

I would like a copy of the brochure, "Picture of Progress," describing Royal Electric.

NAME_____

ROYAL *Electric Typewriter*

Girls who get ahead know why...

They choose clothes, for instance, that do something good for them... clothes to wear at the office, a dress to wear in the evening. Doesn't it make good "get-ahead" sense to choose your office typewriter in the same way?

Royal Electric, too, does something for you as a secretary who believes, "I'm good. I'm going places." Royal is the leading make of typewriter. Surveys show it is the brand preferred $2\frac{1}{4}$ to 1 by girls who type. Designed with you in mind, the Royal Electric Typewriter is newly engineered throughout. Electricity does the work for you! Tension and fatigue are well-nigh banished... and you *feel* better and *look* better, when five o'clock comes.

You'll *love* its operation! The controls are in the same positions as on your favorite Royal Standard Typewriter. There's virtually no "change-over" problem. Who doesn't like being on familiar ground? Now, you ask, how about the work? It pours out... literally. As many as 20 carbon copies, too. Your letters sparkle with a crisp clarity that does you credit. Heavy-duty work is delivered with remarkable speed, ease and efficiency. Exclusive "Touch Control" allows you to adjust the touch to give you the "feel" you prefer. Exclusive "Magic" Margin permits instant, automatic margin setting.

The Royal Electric is *your* typewriter... because of its many exclusive features... because it was designed with *you* in mind. So–do something nice for yourself. Choose Royal.

1952 Sci-Fi Inspired Films

Advertisement

Red Planet Mars by United Artists.   Captive Women by RKO Radio Pictures Inc.

Invasion U.S.A. by Columbia Pictures.   Zombies of the Stratosphere by Republic.

Advertisement

Here's a thought to put in your Easter Bonnet–
For a Treat instead of a Treatment
smoke Old Gold

Let others color their claims with medical talk. But let us remind you: No other leading cigarette is less irritating, or easier on the throat, or contains less nicotine than Old Gold.

This conclusion was established on evidence by the United States Government.

The Chronicles of Narnia   1950–1952

Between 1950 and 1952, children's book author C. S. Lewis published the first three volumes of The Chronicles of Narnia: The Lion, the Witch and the Wardrobe, Prince Caspian and The Voyage of the Dawn Treader.

Set in the fantasy land of Narnia, where children from the real world interact with mythical magical beasts, the books were instantly popular with young readers.

Publisher Geoffrey Bles had feared the books would not sell well. At the time children's books were realistic in nature. Fantasy books were considered inappropriate and potentially harmful to children.

The books became part of a final set of seven books which continue to be international best sellers. They have been translated into 50 languages. The series has been adapted for radio, theater, television, film and video games.

Since 2005, Disney has released a series of three films covering the first three books in sequence.

Musical Memories

Music of the early '50s was smooth and mellow, with lyrics focused on story telling and expressing heartfelt emotion. Classic pop crooners with velvety voices led us to joyous highs and the depths of despair. We had yet to discover the electrifying beats of rock 'n' roll.

Music of the early '50s fell into one of three distinct styles—country, R&B, and pop music. In 1952, there was little cross over between the styles. Radio stations focused on one genre, allowing listeners easy access to their preferred type of music.

One of America's first teen idols, Johnny Ray, dominated the radio airwaves in 1952 with with back-to-back hit singles *Cry* and *The Little White Cloud That Cried*. His overly dramatic stage antics were renowned for provoking the teen hysteria of his fans, years before the phenomenon that was Elvis Presley.

Eddie Fisher and actress Debbie Reynolds at their wedding, 1955.

Teen idol Eddy Fisher released fifteen singles in 1952, in addition to three studio albums. In future years, his good looks and popularity would be overshadowed by his controversial private life. He is now best remembered for his high-profile marriages to actresses Debbie Reynolds and Elizabeth Taylor.

Advertisement

It's a Picnic... Anywhere... with a new Motorola "Town and Country" Portable Radio

All new Motorola portables perform richly where others often fail!

Everybody gathers 'round for that sparkling "Golden Voice" tone... and marvels at the Motorola long-range reception wherever you go! Compact, lightweight cases of weather-resistant plastic or metal—husky, spring-grip handles for easy carrying. Dynamic Alnico V speakers, amazing sensitivity, famous Aerovane Loop or magnetic core antennas for finest reception anywhere. New Concentrated Power chassis, extra long-life battery performance.

- "Town and Country" 3-way styling—Carry it with dial panel tilted open or closed... plays upright or set on its back like a table radio. "Concentrated-Power" AC-DC chassis, longer battery life, exceptional sensitivity and rich "Golden Voice" tone. Green, Gray or Maroon. Model 62L. • "Playmate JR." Armored metal case—Enameled Maroon, Green or Gray metal with a famous Aerovane Loop antenna in the matching flip-up cover. AC, DC, battery reception; automatic battery-saver switch. Model 52M. • "Escort" Amazingly compact— Lots of power and tone quality, yet it's camera size! Extra-durable black Royalite case with strong, silver-color metal trim. Plays upright or rested on handle. AC, DC, battery. Model 52B. • "Escort JR."– Perfect for holiday and vacation fun–a wonderful gift idea! Black and silver-color metal case, powerful tone and reception. Plays upright or on side... battery power only. Model 42B.

New 1952 portable radios priced as low as $24.95!
The "Golden Voice" of radio. Motorola portable radios.

1952 Billboard Top 30 Songs

	Artist	Song Title
1	Leroy Anderson	Blue Tango
2	Kay Starr	Wheel of Fortune
3	Johnnie Ray & The Four Lads	Cry
4	Jo Stafford	You Belong to Me
5	Vera Lynn	Auf Wiederseh'n Sweetheart
6	Rosemary Clooney	Half as Much
7	Eddie Fisher	Wish You Were Here
8	Patti Page	I Went to Your Wedding
9	Al Martino	Here in My Heart
10	Percy Faith	Delicado

Kay Starr.

Eddie Fisher, 1960.

Jo Stafford, 1956.

Patti Page.

	Artist	Song Title
11	Georgia Gibbs	Kiss of Fire
12	Eddie Fisher	Anytime
13	The Four Aces	Tell Me Why
14	Ella Mae Morse	Blacksmith Blues
15	Jo Stafford	Jambalaya (On the Bayou)
16	Rosemary Clooney	Botch-a-Me (Ba-Ba-Baciami Piccina)
17	Doris Day	A Guy Is a Guy
18	Johnnie Ray	The Little White Cloud That Cried
19	Frankie Laine	High Noon
20	Eddie Fisher	I'm Yours

Doris Day, 1957.

Frankie Laine, 1954.

	Artist	Song Title
21	Mills Brothers	The Glow-Worm
22	Johnny Standley	It's in the Book
23	Pee Wee King	Slow Poke
24	Johnnie Ray	Walkin' My Baby Back Home
25	Les Paul	Meet Mister Callaghan
26	Don Cornell	I'm Yours
27	Don Cornell	I'll Walk Alone
28	Eddie Fisher	Tell Me Why
29	The Hilltoppers	Trying
30	Johnnie Ray & The Four Lads	Please, Mr. Sun

* From the *Billboard* top 30 singles of 1952.

Advertisement

PERFECT PAIR! Give one or give both. TIARA—jewel-like alarm...sparkling, dainty, beautiful in the bedroom. IVY—sensational kitchen clock takes real vines. Hangs or stands. Vases color-styled in red, gray, green or yellow. Each **$7.95**

They'll be so proud of your gift if it's a *Telechron®* Electric Clock

GRADUATION GLAMOUR! TRIBUTE! Gift that tells how proud you are! Suntint dial, gold-color base, bell alarm. One of 26 Telechron electric clocks (from $4.95*). No winding, oiling, or regulating. Written warranty. **$10.95**

THEIR VERY OWN! PERSONALITY—most personalized gift you can give. *They* design it (or you can for them!). Slip wedding pictures, mementos, room-matching fabric or wallpaper beneath "crystal." Alarm. **$9.95**

HAPPY HOMECOMING! What a wonderful welcome! A new clock radio with a trustworthy Telechron timer! And what a grand new way to 'wake—with music! Well-known clock radios have Telechron timers.

They'll be so proud of your gift if it's a Telechron Electric Clock

Perfect Pair! Give one or give both. Tiara–jewel like alarm... sparkling, dainty, beautiful in the bedroom. Ivy–sensational kitchen clock takes real vines. Hangs or stands. Vases color-styled in red, gray, green or yellow. Each $7.95.

Graduation Glamour! Tribute! Gift that tells how proud you are! Suntint dial, gold-color base, bell alarm. One of 26 Telechron electric clocks (from $4.95). No winding, oiling, or regulating. Written warranty. $10.95.

Their Very Own! Personality–most personalized gift you can give. *They* design it (or you can for them!). Slip wedding pictures, mementos, room-matching fabric or wallpaper beneath "crystal." Alarm $9.95.

Happy Homecoming! What a wonderful welcome! A new clock radio with a trustworthy Telechron timer! And what a grand new way to wake–with music! Well-known clock radios have Telechron timers.

Advertisement

June Haver danced 28 miles in these Mojud "Magic-Motion" sheer stockings
Magic Motion means extra "give" and spring-back in the knit...the secret of longer wear
Twenty-eight miles of dancing! What colossal punishment for a pair of stockings. "I was worn to a frazzle... but not my Mojuds!" says enchanting June Haver. "I've never seen stockings take such a workout before. These heavenly sheers are sheer heaven to wear!"
No wonder Mojud stockings wear so long, look so glamorous, and fit June Haver's dazzling legs (and yours!) so well. Magic-Motion means extra "give" and spring-back... more cling, and less strain on your stockings when you move.
There are Mojud stockings in wispy sheers, with or without dark seams and glamour heels.
June Haver starring in "the Girl Next Door" 20th Century Fox picture color by Technicolor
Stockings by Mojud

Fashion Trends of the 1950s

With the misery and bleakness of the war years behind us, it was now time to show off. Consumerism was a way of life and we were all too willing to spend money on luxuries, non-essentials, and fashion.

How we looked and how we dressed became important everyday considerations for women and men. We spent money like never before, guided by our favorite fashion icons, and helped along by a maturing advertising industry which flooded us with fashion advice through newspapers, magazines, billboards, radio and television.

1952 Haslams dress fabrics advertisement.

Clothing manufacturers had perfected mass production techniques while providing military uniforms during the war years. They now shifted their focus to well made, stylish, ready-to-wear clothes.

Vogue cover, 1st Aug 1952.

Ebony cover, September 1952.

Australian Home Journal cover, 1st Dec 1952.

Fashion was no longer a luxury reserved for the wealthy. Now the growing middle class could also afford to be fashionable. Magazines and mail-order catalogs kept us informed of the latest trends in fashion, make-up, and accessories.

Advertisement

Dresses from the *Sears* mail order catalog in a mix of the "tea skirt" and "sheath" styles that were popular in the year 1952.

Advertisement

Girdles and bullet bras from the *Sears* mail order catalog in the year 1952.

Christian Dior's "New Look" from 1947.

As with before the war, all eyes looked to Paris for new directions in haute couture. In 1947 Christian Dior didn't disappoint, unveiling his glamorous, extravagant, ultra-feminine "New Look" to the world.

Gone were the boxy tailored jackets with padded shoulders and slim, short skirts. Paris had brought back femininity, with clinched waists, fuller busts and hips, and longer, wider skirts. The emphasis was on abundance. The New Look set the standard for the entire decade of the 1950s.

The "New Look" in the early '50s.

To achieve this impossible hourglass figure, corsets and girdles were sold in record numbers. Metal underwire bras made a comeback, and a new form of bra known as the "cathedral bra" or "bullet bra" became popular.

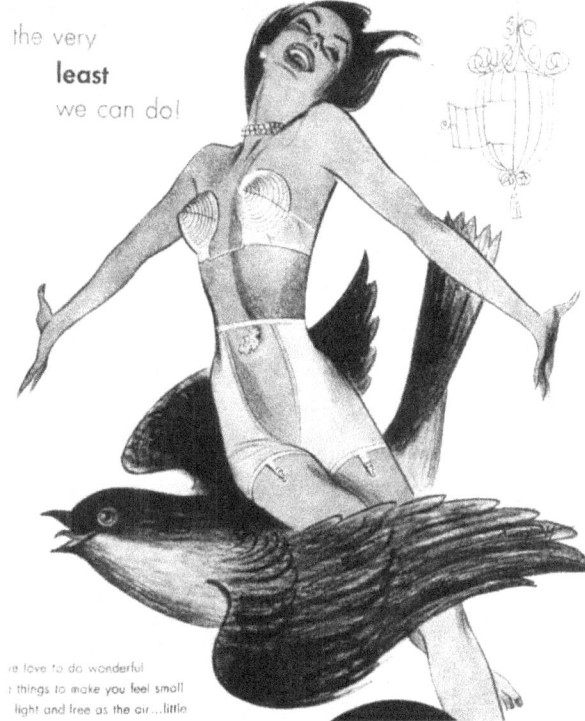

Early '50s bullet bra and girdle from Jantzen.

Despite criticisms against the extravagance of the New Look, and arguments that heavy corsets and paddings undermined the freedoms women had won during the war years, the New Look was embraced on both sides of the Atlantic. Before long, inexpensive, ready-to-wear versions of Dior's New Look had found their way into our department store catalogs.

Butterick Pattern Book, Fall 1952.

Advertisement

LORETTA YOUNG . . . Lustre-Creme presents one of Hollywood's most glamorous stars. Like the majority of top Hollywood stars, Miss Young uses Lustre-Creme Shampoo to care for her beautiful hair

The Most Beautiful Hair in the World
is kept at its loveliest... with Lustre-Creme Shampoo

FAMOUS HOLLYWOOD STARS use LUSTRE-CREME SHAMPOO for GLAMOROUS HAIR

Loretta Young...Lustre-Creme presents one of Hollywood's most glamorous stars. Like the majority of top Hollywood stars, Miss Young uses Lustre-Creme Shampoo to care for her beautiful hair.

The Most Beautiful Hair in the World is kept at its loveliest... with Lustre-Creme Shampoo

When Loretta Young says... "I use Lustre-Creme Shampoo," you're listening to a girl whose beautiful hair plays a vital part in a fabulous glamour-career.

You, too, like Loretta Young, will notice a glorious difference in your hair, after a Lustre-Creme shampoo. Under the spell of its lanolin-blessed lather, your hair shines, behaves, is eager to curl. Hair dulled by soap abuse... dusty with dandruff, now is fragrantly clean. Rebel hair is tamed to respond to the lightest brush touch. Hair robbed of its natural sheen now glows with renewed highlights. Lathers lavishly in hardest water... needs no special after-rinse.

No other cream shampoo in all the world is as popular as Lustre-Creme. For hair that behaves like the angels and shines like the star... ask for Lustre-Creme, the world's finest shampoo, chosen for "the world's most beautiful hair"!

Famous Hollywood Stars use Lustre-Creme Shampoo for Glamorous Hair

Dior also created a slimmed down alternative look, as a sleek dress or elegant straight skirt with short jacket. This figure-hugging, groomed and tailored look, known as the sheath dress, continued to place emphasis on the hourglass figure.

Also known as the "wiggle dress", this sexier figure-hugging silhouette was preferred by movie stars such as Marilyn Monroe.

Women embraced the femininity of 1950s fashion from head to toe. Hats, scarves, belts, gloves, shoes, stockings, handbags and jewelry were all given due consideration.

Out on the street, no outfit would be complete without a full complement of matching accessories.

Not much changed in the world of men's fashion during the 1950s. Business attire shifted just a little. Suits were slimmer, and ties were narrower. Skinny belts were worn over pleated pants. Hats, though still worn, were on the way out.

Marlon Brando.

Frank Sinatra.

James Dean.

For the younger generation however, the fashion icons of the day set the trends. James Dean and Marlon Brando made the white T-shirt and blue jeans the must-have items in casual attire. Worn alone, or under an unbuttoned shirt or jacket, the look made working class style a middle-class fashion statement.

Advertisement

HART SCHAFFNER & MARX
Forecast for Summer–Cool

Our weather forecast for this summer is that it will be uncomfortably warm–but not for the man in a Hart Schaffner & Marx tropical worsted.

Not only will he *feel* cool and confident–he will *look* it. For these, the aristocrats among summer suits, are much more than merely light in weight. They are meticulously tailored. They fit as all really good suits should. They stand out crisply in a crowd. They refuse to yield to heat and humidity. They commend themselves to the man who chooses to be as comfortably well dressed in summer as he is in winter.

The gentleman above is wearing a two-button Bengaline Weave, one of our famous Dixie Weave tropicals. Also available in other models, solid colors and smart patterns.

1952 Olympic Games

February and July 1952

From 14th–25th February, the VI Olympic Winter Games were held in Oslo, Norway, followed by the Games of the XV Olympiad (Summer Olympics) held in Helsinki, Finland from 19th July–3rd August.

Both Games were not without political drama. Held in the aftermath of WWII, with the Cold War and Korean War in full swing, political tensions threatened to cancel the Games completely.

Left: Finnish running legend Paavo Nurmi lights the Olympic fire in Helsinki, 19th July 1952.

Below: Pigeons released during the opening of the Olympics in Helsinki, 19th July 1952.

Both Japan and Germany returned to Olympic competition, having been excluded from the 1948 Games. West Germany attended alone as East Germany declined to participate as a unified German team.

The Soviet Union, Israel, Hong Kong, Thailand, Indonesia (with just three athletes), and the French controlled West German protectorate of Saarland, all made their Olympic debuts. China also made its first Olympic appearance as the People's Republic of China (PROC), then failed to attend another Games until the 1984 Summer Games in Los Angeles, USA. Taiwan withdrew due to the presence of the PROC.

With both the Soviets and Americans planning to attend the Games, security concerns forced Helsinki to construct a second race village to house the Eastern Bloc athletes.

One week before the start of the Winter Olympics, England's King George VI passed away. With Norway's King Haakon VII attending the funeral in London, his granddaughter Princess Ragnhild opened the Games. The British and several Commonwealth team members wore black armbands throughout the Games.

In July, the British were represented at the Summer Games by Queen Elizabeth's husband Prince Philip in one of his first international roles as the Queen's Consort.

Above: Prince Philip and Michael, the Duke of Kent (cousin to Queen Elizabeth II) arrive in Helsinki.

Right: Pole Vaulter at the Summer Games.

Below: Omega, official Olympic timekeepers, record times to the nearest hundredth of a second using their new Electronic Time Recorder, July 1952.

In February, 694 athletes from 30 countries attended the Winter Games to participate in 22 events. Norway won the most medals.

In July, 4,925 athletes from 69 countries participated in 149 events at the Summer Games. The USA won the most medals with 40 gold.

Other Sporting Events from 1952

19th Jan– The Professional Golfers Association (PGA) voted to allow black participants. However, it would be another nine years before Charles Sifford became the first Black golfer to hold a PGA Tour Card.

3rd May– Eddie Arcaro won the 78th Kentucky Derby riding Hill Gail. Arcaro would become an American Hall of Fame jockey, winning more American thoroughbred races than any other jockey in history.

1st July– The first NASCAR Grand National event to be held outside of the US took place at Stamford Park, Ontario, Canada. American Buddy Shuman won the 200-lap race.

4th July– Australian Frank Sedgman won the Wimbledon Men's Singles title marking his fourth Grand Slam win.

5th July– American Maureen Connolly won the Wimbledon Women's Singles title. It would be the first of three consecutive Wimbledon wins for Connolly, and one of nine Grand Slam titles of her short career. Connolly was ranked #1 from 1952-1954, when a freak horse-riding accident ended her tennis career.

3rd Aug– Italian driver Alberto Ascari clinched the Formula 1 World Drivers Championship after eight races, driving for Scuderia Ferrari.

23rd Sept– Rocky Marciano took the heavyweight championship, beating Jersey Joe Walcott in 13 rounds in Philadelphia. Marciano held the title until 1956, when he retired from boxing after 49 undefeated professional fights including 43 knockouts.

Technology and Medicine

3rd May– The De Havilland Comet became the world's first commercial jet airliner with a maiden flight from London to Johannesburg. Technical failures caused three catastrophic crashes within the first year of operation, all due to in-flight break-ups. The plane's square windows were soon changed to a rounded design to avoid metal fatigue at the corners. Rounded windows are standard on all aircraft today.

The first prototype de Havilland DH106 Comet (with square windows) at Hatfield Aerodrome, UK, Oct 1949.

2nd Sep– Dr. F. John Lewis, assisted by Dr. C. Walton Lillehei, performed the world's first open-heart surgery in Minnesota, USA. The patient was a 5-year-old girl.

6th Sep– CBC Toronto and CBC Montreal began the first TV broadcasts in Canada.

1st Dec– The New York Daily News announced the successful sex reassignment surgery for Christine Jorgensen (previously George Jorgensen Jr.) with the headline "Ex-GI Becomes Blonde Beauty". Upon her return from surgery in Copenhagen, Jorgensen became an instant celebrity, with TV, radio and theatre appearances, and the launch of her own nightclub show. Her memoirs sold almost 450,000 copies.

1952– The dreaded polio epidemic peaked in 1952 with 58,000 cases in the USA. More than 3,000 died and 21,000 were left with varying degrees of paralysis. The polio virus, spread by airborne droplets and poor sanitation, mostly affected children. Parents lived in fear, with some implementing extreme social distancing measures. Dr. Jonas Salk began testing his polio vaccine in 1952. The successful trials would lead to a nationwide rollout of the Polio vaccine within three years.

Other News from 1952

3rd Mar– The US Supreme Court upheld a decision to ban Communist teachers from teaching in public schools. The ban would stay in place until 1967, when it was deemed unconstitutional.

10th Mar– A military dictatorship was installed in Cuba following a coup d'état led by General Fulgencio Batista. Canceling the democratic elections due in June, Batista ruled as "Provisional President" for two years, and as elected President for a further 5 years.

5th Apr– Five Norwegian seal hunting vessels carrying a total of 78 men vanish without a trace during a severe storm east of Greenland.

8th Apr– President Harry Truman announced the Government seizure of all steel facilities, to ensure supplies needed for the Korean War. Less than two months later, the Supreme Court ruled that the President did not have executive power to seize private businesses. The steel mills were immediately returned to their owners.

28th Apr– The Treaty of Peace with Japan (or Treaty of San Francisco), formally ended the state of war between the Allied Powers and Japan.

1st May– The Mr. Potato Head toy was released by Hasbro. It was the first toy ever advertised on TV, and the first TV commercial directed exclusively at children. Over one million kits sold in the first year. In the '70s, the size of the toy and parts increased to prevent choking.

Harland Sanders in costume, 1974.

23rd Jul– France, West Germany, Italy, Belgium, Luxembourg and the Netherlands formed the European Coal and Steel community. The organization was the forerunner to the European Union.

24th Sep– Harland (Colonel) Sanders franchised his secret chicken recipe to Pete Harman, and the first "KFC" (Kentucky Fried Chicken) franchise opened in Salt Lake City, Utah.

Rescue workers around wrecked coaches after the Harrow and Wealdstone train crash.

8th Oct– Three trains collided in the UK (Harrow and Wealdstone), killing twelve and injuring 340. It remains the worst peacetime rail crash in the UK.

25th Nov– Agatha Christie's murder-mystery *The Mousetrap* opened at the Ambassadors Theatre, London, later moving to St. Martin's Theatre. It remains the longest running production of a play in history.

2nd Dec– Venezuela's military junta canceled the country's elections and declared their leader, Colonel Perez Jimenez, the Provisional President. Jimenez ruled as dictator until 1958.

1952- Mother Teresa, committed to helping "the poorest of the poor", opened her first hospice–a home for the dying and destitute in Calcutta. (Photo 1986).

Advertisement

Real "He-Man" Eating!
(Easy to Make–at a price easy to take–thanks to Ann Page)

There's no end to the wonderful ways you can serve Ann Page Macaroni... with fish– as in this "Seaflake Macaroni Bake"... or serve it with cheese... with vegetables... with sauces. Every dish delicious, thanks to Ann Page Fancy Semolina Macaroni that cooks up firm yet tender. Try it... there's none better at any price!

You'll like the other fine foods in the Ann Page "family of 33" too. All made of choice ingredients in A&P's own modern food kitchens and sold in A&P stores. This eliminates unnecessary in-between expenses and you share the savings.

Among the 33 Fine Foods in the Famous Ann Page Family are such favorites as: Preserves, Peanut Butter, Prepared Beans, Prepared Spaghetti, Salad Dressing, Mayonnaise, Sparkle Gelatin Desserts and Puddings, Tomato Soup, Ketchup, Spices, Extracts, Etc.

Advertisement

Warriors against Death

Have you ever stood anxiously at the sickbed of your child? Watched your doctor give one of the "miracle" drugs? Seen, within hours, the puckered frown of pain dissolve into a grin?

Perhaps you've wondered, thankfully, who made these drugs possible. You can look to the men and women of good will in the laboratories at universities, hospitals and the great pharmaceutical houses.

They are a strange breed. Quiet, shy — not much on talk. Their reward is far beyond that of money. These dedicated scientists have the immense spiritual satisfaction of helping to heal human misery. They hate disease. They fight the daily presence of Death.

Spread over the 400 rolling acres at Lederle Laboratories is one of the most important groups of medical-research men and women in the world. No other group in the pharmaceutical field can rely upon better facilities than are found here.

From here come the child-saving biologicals. Here sulfadiazine — the giant among sulfas — was tested. Here was discovered the lifesaving, golden colored drug, aureomycin — recognized as one of the most versatile disease-killers known today.

A thimbleful of crystals may be the first world supply of such a new drug. Lederle employs its vast resources to turn this thimbleful into millions of capsules; so that doctors in the small town, and in the great city, share equally the latest discoveries for preserving health and saving life.

Lederle—dedicated to helping your doctor help you **live**

LEDERLE LABORATORIES DIVISION
AMERICAN *Cyanamid* COMPANY
30 Rockefeller Plaza, New York 20, N. Y.

Famous People Born in 1952

16th Jan– Fuad II of Egypt, last King of Egypt & Sudan (1952-'53), Head of Royal House of Egypt (1965-).

2nd Feb– Park Geun-hye, 1st female President of South Korea (2013-2017).

10th Feb– Lee Hsien Loong, Prime Minister of Singapore (People's Action Party: 2004-).

19th March– Harvey Weinstein, American film producer (Miramax) & convicted sex offender.

23rd March– Rex Tillerson, American businessman (ExxonMobil) & US Secretary of State (2017-18).

24th Apr– Jean Paul Gaultier, French fashion designer.

16th Apr– Bill Belichick, American NFL coach (6x Super Bowl 2002-'18).

2nd May– Christine Baranski, American stage & screen actress.

15th May– David Brandon, American exec. (Domino's Pizza, Toys "R" Us CEO).

21st May– Mr. T. (Lawrence Tureaud), American actor.

7th Jun– Liam Neeson, Irish-American actor.

18th Jun– Isabella Rossellini, Italian actress & model.

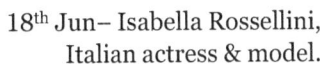

25th Jun– Tim Finn, New Zealand singer, songwriter & musician (Split Enz).

1st Jul– Dan Aykroyd, Canadian-American comedian, writer & actor.

17th Jul– David Hasselhoff, American actor.

5th Aug– Hun Sen, Cambodian politician, Prime Minister of Cambodia (1985-).

5th Aug– Louis Walsh, Irish music manager & TV personality.

17th Aug– Guillermo Vilas, Argentine tennis player (4x Grand Slam winner).

18th Aug– Patrick Swayze, American actor & dancer (d.2009).

27th Aug– Pee-wee Herman (Paul Reubens), American comic actor (d. 2023).

2nd Sep– Jimmy Connors, American tennis player (8x Grand Slam winner).

9th Sep– Angela Cartwright, British-American actress.

9th Sep– David Stewart, guitarist, songwriter & producer (Eurythmics).

25th Sep– Christopher Reeve, American actor (d.2004).

5th Oct– Imran Khan, 22nd Prime Minister of Pakistan (2018-) & cricket all-rounder (88 Tests).

7th Oct– Vladimir Putin, Russian politician (President & Prime Minister).

9th Oct– Sharon Osbourne, English-American TV personality.

22nd Oct– Jeff Goldblum, American actor.

27th Oct– Roberto Benigni, Italian director & actor.

3rd Nov– Roseanne Barr, American comedienne & TV personality.

16th Nov– Shigeru Miyamoto, Japanese video game designer (Nintendo, Mario).

10th Dec– Susan Dey, American actress.

27th Dec– David Knopfler, British singer-songwriter (Dire Straits).

Advertisement

give yourself a coffee-break

...and get what coffee gives to you!

coffee always gives you a break!

Think Better!... At Republic Aviation Corporation, test pilot Lyle Monkton, a "scientist of the sky," gets ready to test another Republic Thunderjet... and takes a coffee-break! A cup of fragrant coffee gently stimulates your mind... helps you when you have to think fast. A *delicious* aid to clearer thinking... is a coffee-break!

Give yourself a coffee-break... and get what coffee gives to you!
Coffee always give you a break!

Work Better!... Republic's ground crew tunes up the new fighter-bomber—and has a coffee-break! Coffee's gentle lift helps ease fatigue, helps you feel more alert. Whatever job you have to do—do yourself a favor. Take a coffee-break!

Feel Better!... The gang builds a jet plane, too—scale model size—and takes a coffee-break! A cup of full-strength coffee adds fun to everything you do. So pour a cheerful cup, several times a day. Give yourself a coffee-break!

Drink it often!... Enjoy coffee at mealtimes. Relax with coffee in-between—at home, at work, or in your favorite restaurant. In fact, wouldn't *right now* be a swell time... for a coffee-break?

Pan-American Coffee Bureau. 120 Wall St., New York 5 • Brazil • Colombia • Costa Rica • Cuba • Dominican Republic • Ecuador • El Salvador • Guatemala • Honduras • Mexico • Venezuela

1952 in Numbers

Census Statistics [1]:

- Population of the world   2.63 billion
- Population in the United States   163.27 million
- Population in the United Kingdom   50.65 million
- Population in Canada   14.45 million
- Population in Australia   8.59 million
- Average age for marriage of women   20.2 years old
- Average age for marriage of men   23.0 years old
- Average family income USA $3,900 per year
- Unemployment rate USA   2.7 %

Costs of Goods [2]:

- Average new house — $9,050
- Average new car — $1,700
- New Jaguar XK120 — $5,065
- A gallon of gasoline — $0.27
- Butter — $0.77 per pound
- A loaf of bread — $0.12
- Peanut butter — $0.29
- Beef, ribs — $0.69 per pound
- Oranges, Florida — $0.29 per 5 pounds
- Sliced bacon — $0.55 per pound
- Eggs — $0.55 per dozen
- Ketchup, 14oz bottle — $0.19
- Toilet paper, Scott — $0.25 per 2 rolls
- Newspaper, Daily Record — $0.50

---

1 Figures taken from worldometers.info/world-population, US National Center for Health Statistics, Divorce and Divorce Rates US (cdc.gov/nchs/data/series/sr_21/sr21_029.pdf) and United States Census Bureau, Historical Marital Status Tables (census.gov/data/tables/time-series/demo/families/marital.html).

2 Figures from thepeoplehistory.com and mclib.info/reference/local-history-genealogy/historic-prices/.

Advertisement

Marilyn Monroe discovers the world's most glamorous make-up... from the Westmores of Hollywood

You can share the wizardry of the world's foremost beauty experts, the men who make the stars more beautiful; Pere Westmore, the dean of Hollywood make-up artists; Wally Westmore, Make-up Director, Paramount Studios; Frank Westmore, famous Hollywood make-up stylist; Bud Westmore, Make-up Director, Universal Studios.

The world's most glamorous stars asked for it... an *easier-to-apply, longer-lasting* make-up that would give them the same complexion glamor on the street that they have in close-ups on the screen! And the Westmores gave it to them... fabulous liquid Tru-Glo! A make-up that literally flows on your cheek.

You just dot it on, blend evenly with your fingertips, and pat off excess with a tissue. Presto! Your complexion takes on a luminous freshness–a petal-softness–that lasts all day!

Tru-Glo hides tattle-tale lines and imperfections... draws a sheer veil of color over blemishes... gives you a truly poreless look! Even more important, it imparts a radiant natural glow that brings out your true beauty!

And... satiny Tru-Glo never streaks. Never leaves a "masky" look. Not greasy or drying. The world's most glamorous make-up, magical Tru-Glo gives you breath-taking loveliness!

Acclaimed by Hollywood Tru-Glo liquid make-up only 59¢ plus tax.

Advertisement

"fresh up" with Seven-Up!
The all-family drink!

Bright and lively as a baby on the beach...chilled 7-Up goes with a summer day like a dip in the waves. So pure...so good...so wholesome that big folks, small folks, *all* folks can "fresh up" as often as they like. When the sun's high and your throat's dry–reach for sparkling, crystal-clear 7-Up!

Buy it by the case or in the new light and handy 7-Up family pack of 24 bottles! Easy-lift center handle! Space saving! Family supply!

These words first appeared in print in the year 1952.

- DEEP SPACE
- cop out
- standard operating procedure
- Junk food
- capri pants
- stress fracture
- defibrillator
- Photo opportunity
- Hawaiian shirt
- Global warming
- do-it-yourself
- sonic boom
- mind-bending
- modem
- underachiever
- SWING STATE
- Veterans Day

*From merriam-webster.com/time-traveler/1952.

A heartfelt plea from the author:

I sincerely hope you enjoyed reading this book and that it brought back many fond memories from the past.

Success as an author has become increasingly difficult with the proliferation of **AI generated** copycat books by unscrupulous sellers. They are clever enough to escape copyright action and use dark web tactics to secure paid-for **fake reviews**, something I would never do.

Hence I would like to ask you—I plead with you—the reader, to leave a star rating or review on Amazon. This helps make my book discoverable for new readers, and helps me to compete fairly against the devious copycats.

If this book was a gift to you, you can leave stars or a review on your own Amazon account, or you can ask the gift-giver or a family member to do this on your behalf.

I have enjoyed researching and writing this book for you and would greatly appreciate your feedback.

Best regards,
Bernard Bradforsand-Tyler.

Please leave a
book review/rating at:

https://bit.ly/1952-reviews

Or scan the QR code:

Flashback books make the perfect gift- see the full range at

https://bit.ly/FlashbackSeries

Image Attributions

Photographs and images used in this book are reproduced courtesy of the following:

Page 6 – From *Life* Magazine 1st Dec 1952.
Source: books.google.com/books?id=tlIEAAAAMBAJ&printsec (PD image).*
Page 8 – From *Life* Magazine 14th Apr 1952.
Source: books.google.com/books?id=9FUEAAAAMBAJ&printsec (PD image).*
Page 9 – From *Life* Magazine 9th Jun 1952.
Source: books.google.com/books?id=6FUEAAAAMBAJ&printsec (PD image).*
Page 10 – From *Life* Magazine 8th Sep 1952.
Source: books.google.com/books?id=flYEAAAAMBAJ&printsec (PD image).*
Page 11 – From *Life* Magazine 6th Oct 1952. Source: books.google.com/books?id=uVIEAAAAMBAJ& printsec (PD image).* – Magazine cover by Science Service Inc. Source: comicbookplus.com/?cbplus= atomic. Pre 1978, no mark (PD image).
Page 12 – From *Life* Magazine 16th Jun 1952.
Source: books.google.com/books?id=2lUEAAAAMBAJ&printsec (PD image).*
Page 13 – Queen Elizabeth & Probir Sen at Lord's Cricket Ground by Abhijit Sen. Source: search.creative commons.org/photos/3d631476-f436-4609-86b4-875edda5c618. License CC BY-SA 3.0 (PD image).
Page 14 – London aerial by Sunshine34, commons.wikimedia.org/wiki/File:London_1953.jpg. License CC BY-SA 3.0 (PD image). – Classroom photo, Creator unknown. Pre 1978, no mark (PD image).
Page 15 – Truman & Churchill, 20th Mar 1952 from the US Library of Congress. LOC Control Number 96519550 (PD image).
Page 16 – From *Life* Magazine 10th Mar 1952.
Source: books.google.com/books?id=eFQEAAAAMBAJ&printsec (PD image).*
Page 17 – King George V1, photographer unknown, circa 1942. From the US Library of Congress. US Government owned. Reproduction Number: LC-USW33-019073-C (PD image). – Queen Elizabeth II, photographer unknown, 1959. From the Library Archives of Canada, reproduction number: e010975985. Attribution 4.0 International (CC BY 4.0).
Page 18 – From *Life* Magazine 19th May 1952. Source: books.google.com/books?id=G1YEAAAAMBAJ& printsec (PD image).*
Page 19 – Cadillac print advertisement, 1952. Source: eBay (PD image).*
Page 20 – Traffic, creator unknown. Source: theoldmotor.com/?p=171594. Pre 1978, (PD image).*
Page 21 – Hudson Hornet Hollywood Hardtop (1952) Source: flickr.com/photos/andreboeni/ 39970044972 by Andrew Bone. Attribution 4.0 Int (CC BY 4.0). – Mercury 1952 Hardtop from *Life* Magazine 6th Oct 1952. Source: books.google.com.sg/books?id=uVIEAAAAMBAJ&printsec (PD image).*
Page 22 – From *Life* Magazine 14th Jan 1952.
Source: books.google.com/books?id=mVQEAAAAMBAJ&printsec (PD image).*
Page 23 – Lincoln print advertisement, 1952. Source: eBay (PD image).*
Page 24 – From *Life* Magazine 21st Apr and 19th May 1952. Source: books.google.com/books?id= 2VUEAAAAMBAJ&printsec and books.google.com/books?id=G1YEAAAAMBAJ&printsec (PD image).*
Page 25 – Screen still from *The Colgate Comedy Hour*, by Colgate-Palmolive-Peet.** Source: commons. wikimedia.org/wiki/File:Dean_Martin_Jerry_Lewis_Colgate_Comedy_Hour_early_1950s.JPG. – Screen still from *Dragnet*, NBC Television** 30th August 1957,
source: en.wikipedia.org/wiki/Dragnet_(1951_TV_series).
Page 26 – From *Life* Magazine 14th Jan 1952.
Source: books.google.com/books?id=mVQEAAAAMBAJ&printsec (PD image).*
Page 27 – Show dancers, *American Bandstand* screen still by WFIL.** Date unknown. – *The Guiding Light* premiere show 30th June 1952 screen still.** Source: latimes.com/entertainment/guiding-light-moments-photogallery.html. – *This is Your Life,* screen still 20th August 1954 by NBC.**
Source: en.wikipedia.org/wiki/This_Is_Your_Life. – *The Today Show* publicity photo 26th November 1954 by NBC. Source: en.wikipedia.org/wiki/Today_(American_TV_program).
Page 28 – From Life Magazine 1st Dec 1962.
Source: books.google.com/books?id=tlIEAAAAMBAJ&printsec (PD image).*
Page 29 – Garroway, photo by Macfadden Publishing, cropped from TV Radio Mirror magazine, page 55. Source: commons.wikimedia.org/wiki/File:Dave_Garroway_signoff_of_Peace.jpg. – Garroway and crew on The Today Show set, 1952, by Radio Corporation of America. Both images this page are pre-1978, no copyright marks (PD images).
Page 30 – From Life Magazine 12th May 1962. Source: books.google.com/books?id=HFYEAAAAMBAJ &printsec (PD image).*
Page 31 – Ivy Mike by The Official CTBTO, source: flickr.com/photos/ctbto/ 6476282811/. Pre 1978, no copyright mark (PD image). – Las Vegas tourism postcard from the early '50s, creator unknown. Pre 1978, no copyright mark (PD image).

Page 32 & 33 – Medical Corpsmen helping wounded, 14th Oct 1952. Signal Corps Photo #1-4885-4/FEC-52-30954 (Sylvester). – USMC M-46 Patton Medium Tank by TSGT. U.S. Marine Corps, (NARA FILE #: 127-GK-233P-A163131). 8th July 1952. – Helicopter in Korea, 1953, by PFC E. E. Green, U.S. Army - NARA FILE#: 111-SC-422077. – VF-11 F2H-2 over Wonsan, 20th Oct 1952. Official U.S. Navy photo 80-G-480436 from the U.S. Navy Naval History and Heritage Command. – Korean girl carrying her brother, by Maj. R.V. Spencer, UAF (Navy), 8th June 1951. From the National Archives and Records Administration, National Archives Identifier (NAID) 520796. Source: commons.wikimedia.org/wiki/Korean_ War. All photos these pages are the work of US Army Soldiers, US Marines or their employees and are in the public domain.

Page 34 – Big Ben photo taken during the Great Smog, creator unknown. – Battersea Power Station, source: en.wikipedia.org/wiki/File:Battersea_power_station_1950.jpg. Both images pre 1978, no copyright mark (PD image).

Page 35 – Houses of Parliament, Source: commons.wikimedia.org/wiki/File:Houses_of_Parliament_and_ Big_Ben.png. Licenced under Creative Commons Attribution-Share Alike 3.0 Unported.

Page 36 – From *Life* Magazine 28th July 1952.
Source: books.google.com/books?id=3VUEAAAAMBAJ&printsec (PD image).*

Page 37 – Nassar and Naguib, source: en.wikipedia.org/wiki/Gamal_Abdel_Nasser#Revolution. (PD images).

Page 38 – Danger Sign, reproduction of a farm sign in Johannesburg. 1st July 1952.
Source: commons.wikimedia.org/wiki/ Category:Apartheid_signage (PD image). – Photo from timeslive.co.za, photographer unknown. (PD image).

Page 39 – Photo from sahistory.org.za, photographer unknown. Pre 1978, no mark (PD image).
– Photo from religiousleftlaw.com, photographer unknown. Pre 1978, no copyright mark (PD image).

Page 40 – From *Life* Magazine 20th Oct 1952.
Source: books.google.com/books?id=21IEAAAAMBAJ&printsec (PD image).*

Page 41 – From *Life* Magazine 19th May 1952.
Source: books.google.com/books?id=G1YEAAAAMBAJ&printsec (PD image).*

Page 42 – Screen still from *The Greatest Show on Earth*, by Paramount Pictures 1952.** Source: commons. wikimedia.org/wiki/Category:The_Greatest_Show_on_Earth_(film). – Still image from video of *The Redbook Awards*, 1953.** – Bridgitte Bardot, source: flickr.com/photos/classicvintage/ 9274563680. Attribution 4.0 International (CC BY 4.0).

Page 43 – *The Snows of Kilimanjaro*, 1952 film poster by 20th Century Fox.** – *The Greatest Show on Earth*, 1952 film poster by Paramount Pictures.** – *Singin' in the Rain*, 1952 film poster by MGM.**

Page 44 – From *Life* Magazine 4th Feb 1952.
Source: books.google.com/books?id=fVQEAAAAMBAJ&printsec (PD image).*

Page 45 – *Red Planet Mars*, 1952 movie poster by United Artists.** Source: en.wikipedia.org/wiki/Red_ Planet _Mars. – *Captive Woman*, 1952 movie poster by RKO Radio Pictures Inc.**
Source: en.wikipedia.org/wiki/ Captive_Women. – *Invasion U.S.A.*, 1952 movie poster by Columbia Pictures.** Source: en.wikipedia.org/wiki/Invasion,_U.S.A._(1952_film). – *Zombies of the Stratosphere*, 1952 movie poster by Republic.** Source: en.wikipedia.org/wiki/Zombies_of_the_ Stratosphere.

Page 46 – From *Life* Magazine 7th Apr 1952.
Source: books.google.com/books?id=EIYEAAAAMBAJ&printsec (PD image).*

Page 47 – Book cover and film posters.**
Source: en.wikipedia.org/wiki/The_Lion,_the_Witch_and_the_Wardrobe.

Page 48 – Johnnie Ray studio portrait 1950, creator unknown. Pre 1978, no copyright mark (PD image).
– Wedding of Fisher and Reynolds, 1955, creator unknown.
Source: commons.wikimedia.org/wiki/Category:Eddie_Fisher (PD image).

Page 49 – From *Life* Magazine 26th May 1952.
Source: books.google.com/books?id=C1YEAAAAMBAJ&printsec (PD image).*

Page 50 – Kay Starr, studio publicity photo, Source: en.wikipedia.org/wiki/Kay_Starr. – Eddie Fisher studio publicity photo, source: commons.wikimedia.org/wiki/Category:Eddie_Fisher. – Jo Stafford, by Colombia Records Feb 1956. Source: commons.wikimedia.org/wiki/File:Jo_Stafford_1956.JPG. – Patti Page source: wikivisually.com/wiki/Patti_Page by General Artists Corporation. All images this page permission PD-PRE1978.

Page 51 – Doris Day promotional photo, 1957. Source: en.wikipedia.org/wiki/Doris_Day. PD-PRE1978 (PD image). – Frankie Laine publicity photo, 1954. Source: en.wikipedia.org/wiki/Frankie_Laine. PD-PRE1978 (PD image).

Page 52 – From *Life* Magazine 19th May 1952.
Source: books.google.com/books?id=G1YEAAAAMBAJ&printsec (PD image).*

Page 53 – From *Life* Magazine 7th Apr 1952.
Source: books.google.com/books?id=EIYEAAAAMBAJ&printsec (PD image).*

Page 54 – Advertisement for Haslams dress fabrics, 1952.
Source: likesoldclothes.tumblr.com/tagged/1952/ (PD image).*

Page 55 – Fashion magazine covers from 1952. Pre 1978, no copyright mark (PD image).*

Pages 56 & 57 – Sears Catalog 1952, source: snapped-garters.blogspot.com/2014/06/1952-fashions-from-sears.html (PD images).*

Page 58 – Photo by Lars Nordin, Source:commons.wikimedia.org/w/index.php?curid=39208366. Attribution: CC BY 4.0.
Page 59 – Butterick cover, Fall 1952. Source: likesoldclothes.tumblr.com/tagged/1952/. Pre 1978 (PD image).* – Jantzen advert. Source: flickr.com/photos/nesster/5521936717/ Attribution 4.0 International (CC BY 4.0).
Page 60 – From *Life* Magazine 25th Aug 1952.
Source: books.google.com/books?id=g1YEAAAAMBAJ&printsec (PD image).*
Page 61 – Marilyn Monroe in 1952 studio publicity portrait for film Niagara, by 20th Century Fox. (PD image). – Models walking photo. Source: Jessica at myvintagevogue.com. Licensed under CC BY 2.0.
Page 62 – Sinatra, source: morrisonhotelgallery.com/collections/wtvp8g/The-Sinatra-Experience-. – Brando, source: dailybreak.co/wp-content/uploads/2019/06/Marlon-Brando-Ford-Thunderbird-1955-Est.-2444.jpg. – Dean, source: en.wikipedia.org/wiki/James_Dean. All images this page Pre-1978, no copyright mark (PD image).
Page 63 – From *Life* Magazine 5th May 1952.
Source: books.google.com/books?id=HVYEAAAAMBAJ&printsec (PD image).*
Page 64 & 65 – Images from the Summer Olympics of 1952. Source: commons.wikimedia.org/wiki/Category: 1952_ Summer_Olympics. All images are in the Public Domain.
Page 66 – Eddie Arcaro in 1957. Source: commons.wikimedia.org/wiki/File:Jayne_Mansfield_ with_jockeys_ in_1957.jpg (cropped). – Maureen Connolly, source: commons.wikimedia.org/wiki/ Category:Maureen_ Connolly. – Rocky Marciano, source: commons.wikimedia.org/wiki/Category: Rocky_Marciano. All photos this page are in the Public Domain.
Page 67 – Comet 1 by British official photographer - ATP 18376C from the collections of the Imperial War Museums. Source: iwm.org.uk/collections/item/object/205126073. (PD image).
– Christine Jorgensen by Maurice Seymour, New York, 1954.
Source: commons.wikimedia.org/wiki/Category:Christine_Jorgensen. (PD image).
Page 68 – Batista, 1952. Source: commons.wikimedia.org/wiki/Category:Fulgencio_Batista (PD image).
– Truman, 16th Dec 1950, from the National Archives and Records Administration (NAID) 541951. Source: en.wikipedia.org/wiki/Presidency_ of_Harry_S._Truman. US Federal Government photo (PD image). – Original Mr Potato Head boxed set. Source: en.wikipedia.org/wiki/Mr._Potato_Head. Photo included for information only under US fair use laws due to: 1- image is low resolution copy, too small to be used to make illegal copies for use in another book; 2- image does not devalue the ability of the copyright holder to profit from the original work in any way; 3- The image is relevant to the article created.
Page 69 – Harland Sanders, 1974. Source: commons.wikimedia.org/wiki/Category:Harland_Sanders. Copyright attribution CC BY-SA 3.0. – Rescue workers around wrecked coaches after the Harrow and Wealdstone train crash, 8th Oct 1952. Source: railwaysarchive.co.uk/documents/MoT_Harrow001.pdf (PD image). – Mother Teresa in Bonn, Germany, 1986. Source: commons.wikimedia.org/wiki/Category:Mother_Teresa. Copyright attribution CC BY-SA 2.0 de.
Page 70 – From *Life* Magazine 3rd Mar 1952.
Source: books.google.com/books?id=cFQEAAAAMBAJ&printsec (PD image).*
Page 71 – From *Life* Magazine 7th Apr 1952.
Source: books.google.com/books?id=EIYEAAAAMBAJ&printsec (PD image).*
Page 72-74 – All photos are, where possible, CC BY 2.0 or PD images made available by the creator for free use including commercial use. Where commercial use photos are unavailable, photos are included here for information only under US fair use laws due to: 1- images are low resolution copies; 2- images do not devalue the ability of the copyright holders to profit from the original works in any way; 3- Images are too small to be used to make illegal copies for use in another book; 4- The images are relevant to the article created.
Page 75 – From *Life* Magazine 10th Nov 1952.
Source: books.google.com/books?id=1IIEAAAAMBAJ&printsec (PD image).*
Page 78 – From *Life* Magazine 13th Oct 1952.
Source: books.google.com/books?id=3IIEAAAAMBAJ&printsec (PD image).*
Page 79 – 7-Up print magazine advertisement. Pre 1978, no copyright mark (PD image).

*Advertisement (or image from an advertisement) is in the public domain because it was published in a collective work (such as a periodical issue) in the US between 1925 and 1977 and without a copyright notice specific to the advertisement.
**Posters for movies or events are either in the public domain (published in the US between 1925 and 1977 and without a copyright notice specific to the artwork) or owned by the production company, creator, or distributor of the movie or event. Posters, where not in the public domain, and screen stills from movies or TV shows, are reproduced here under USA Fair Use laws due to: 1- images are low resolution copies; 2- images do not devalue the ability of the copyright holders to profit from the original works in any way; 3- Images are too small to be used to make illegal copies for use in another book; 4- The images are relevant to the article created.

This book was written by Bernard Bradforsand-Tyler as part of *A Time Traveler's Guide* series of books.

All rights reserved. The author exerts the moral right to be identified as the author of the work.

No parts of this book may be reproduced, stored in any retrieval system, or transmitted in any form or by any means, without prior written permission from the author.

This is a work of nonfiction. No names have been changed, no events have been fabricated. The content of this book is provided as a source of information for the reader, however it is not meant as a substitute for direct expert opinion. Although the author has made every effort to ensure that the information in this book is correct at time of printing, and while this publication is designed to provide accurate information in regard to the subject matters covered, the author assumes no responsibility for errors, inaccuracies, omissions, or any other inconsistencies herein and hereby disclaims any liability to any party for any loss, damage, or disruption caused by errors or omissions.

All images contained herein are reproduced with the following permissions:
- Images included in the public domain.
- Images obtained under creative commons license.
- Images included under fair use terms.
- Images reproduced with owner's permission.

All image attributions and source credits are provided at the back of the book. All images are the property of their respective owners and are protected under international copyright laws.

First printed in 2022 in the USA (ISBN 978-1-922676-02-3).
Revised in 2024, 2nd Edition (978-1-922676-21-4).
Self-published by B. Bradforsand-Tyler.

www.ingramcontent.com/pod-product-compliance
Lightning Source LLC
Chambersburg PA
CBHW072104110526
44590CB00018B/3308